## COMPANION WORKBOOK

### Empower Yourself to Live a Happier, More Fulfilling Life

# FEELING

# STUCK?

## — 10 TENETS OF —
## Mindset Transformation Coaching®

# NICOLE HOLLAR

Mindset Press, LLC

ISBN: 979-8-9883168-0-0 (Paperback)

ISBN: 979-8-9883168-1-7 (eBook)

Editor: Katrina Nichols

Cover designer: Klassic Designs

Interior workbook layout: Nicole Hollar

Visit the author's website for purchases, bookings, and workshops:

www.nicolehollar.com

support@nicolehollar.com

# CONTENTS

This Companion Workbook to "FEELING STUCK?" asks you questions and gives you exercises and tools to apply the concepts you learn with each of the **10 Tenets of Mindset Transformation.** These are the same style and types of questions I ask private one-to-one Mindset Transformation Coaching® clients, and I want you to have full access to the entire program. Consider these exercises as tools to help you grow; they are your homework. As you move through the workbook, really think through the questions or engage in the exercise as described. The more input you give the more you will get from your coaching program.

## 10 Tenets of Mindset Transformation

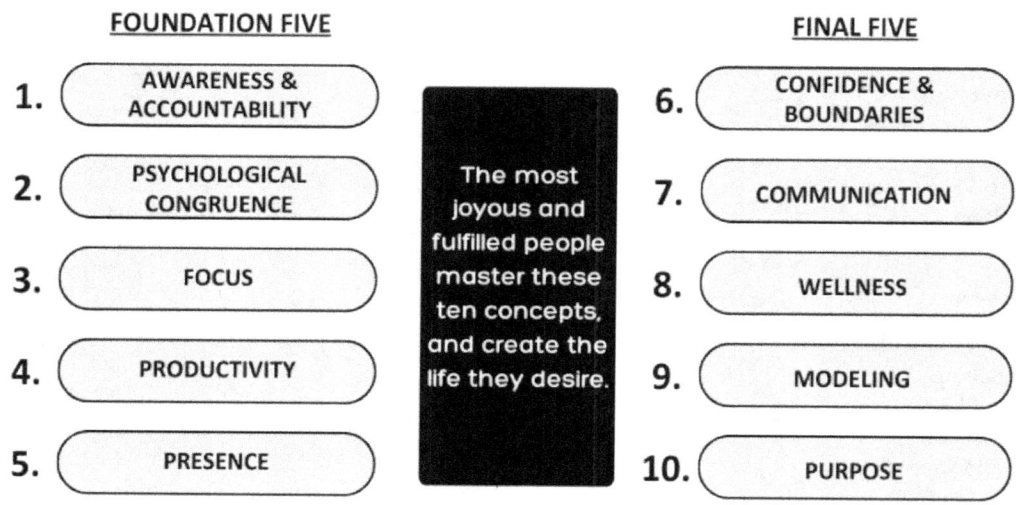

| FOUNDATION FIVE | | FINAL FIVE |
|---|---|---|
| 1. AWARENESS & ACCOUNTABILITY | The most joyous and fulfilled people master these ten concepts, and create the life they desire. | 6. CONFIDENCE & BOUNDARIES |
| 2. PSYCHOLOGICAL CONGRUENCE | | 7. COMMUNICATION |
| 3. FOCUS | | 8. WELLNESS |
| 4. PRODUCTIVITY | | 9. MODELING |
| 5. PRESENCE | | 10. PURPOSE |

# HOW TO USE THE WORKBOOK

The deeper you dig the more you will uncover, learn, and grow. The exercises in this workbook are meant to be used in tandem with "FEELING STUCK?". Without reading the book the exercises may not make as much sense nor be as effective. I recommend learning about each tenet in "FEELING STUCK?" and then doing its companion exercises so that all of your learning is fresh and helps you create more positive momentum. Refer to the book to get clarity on things you noticed, want to take action on, and anything new you learned.

Take any additional notes you believe will be helpful and consider this workbook a journal where you can reflect on your responses and determine the next steps that are appropriate for you.

**You can purchase your copy of "FEELING STUCK? Empower Yourself to Live a Happier, More Fulfilling Life" at Amazon.com if you have not already. Scan QR code for direct access.**

# PREPARING YOUR MINDSET

As you move forward, I want you to ask yourself what your number one focus is for your coaching program. Maybe you want to build more confidence, learn to put yourself first and have better and more meaningful conversations and relationships. Do you give your full effort at work and feel like it's never enough? Maybe you are hoping to learn tools to better manage time or people, or to help you be more efficient by having better boundaries. Whatever your specific goal, know you are totally capable of feeling better, having more enthusiasm, and a better quality of life.

Now, if you already have a general sense of which area you want to focus on, I'd like you to do some quick exploration. Even if you are not sure just yet, let the first voice that comes into your head be the thing you write down for each question. Honor what that little voice has said. Don't judge or question it. Just write it down. If you need to dive deeper later, you absolutely can.

1.  Think about areas of your life like career, family, relationships, self, or health. Where are you unfulfilled, or not showing up as your best self? Why? What could you do about it?

In "FEELING STUCK?" I talked about how you often need to eliminate a thought or behavior to make room for what would give you effective change.

2.  Now as you think about this area of your life, what will you need to do or stop doing to see improvement? Whatever you thought is terrific. Write it down.

3. Will improving this area of life make the most impact on all other areas? What will happen when you make the necessary changes?

........................................................................................................................

........................................................................................................................

........................................................................................................................

4. What has held you back from making those changes?

........................................................................................................................

........................................................................................................................

........................................................................................................................

Why now?

........................................................................................................................

........................................................................................................................

........................................................................................................................

5. Finally, what 2-4 things could you do differently to manage this better?

........................................................................................................................

........................................................................................................................

........................................................................................................................

Thinking through those questions and writing them down means you are already off to a great start. The primary feedback I get from clients who answer those questions is the realization that people don't do a check-in often enough, or that they realize they are waiting for the world to shift in order to have everything fall into place, rather than acting from a place of empowerment.

As you move into the core of the program, you'll have homework based on each tenet. The beginning will start you thinking and recognizing areas where you are doing awesome and other areas where you can improve, and you'll probably have a few "ah ha" moments along the way.

You are just getting started and doing great by coming this far. You are well on your way to improving not only your life, but those around you either directly or by modeling.

# TENET 1
# AWARENESS & ACCOUNTABILITY

**Themes:**

- Taking an honest look at yourself, values, judgments, obstacles and how you manage them, your personal accountability, and your "why," the reason you desire MORE from life.
- Evaluating your current focus on each area of the Sectors of Self.
- Uncovering your most critical values for one or more of the Sectors of Self.

**Exercise Topics:** *The Honesty Chart, Sectors of Self, Values Elicitation*

# The Honesty Chart

To complete the Honesty Chart in a way that gives you the most value, below are things to consider as you complete the exercise that follows.

## SELF

Since your coaching is all about you, let's start with the most essential area of the Honesty Chart: Self. Getting to know yourself better by looking inward and learning to be okay with whatever you see and feel is an essential part of positive growth.

The first thing I ask about is the favorable words you would use to describe yourself. Please keep this in mind, I am looking for words that both you and other people believe to be true. You see, we can all think very highly of ourselves because in our mind that's who we think we are or want to be, but sometimes that's not what we show.

Let me give you an example, a word I have often heard people want to describe themselves is "thoughtful." In this case, I might ask what that means to them and often it is that they literally "think" of a person or people. Here's the catch, are you only thoughtful of a single person? Do you *act* on those thoughts and are present, helpful, and giving? Ask yourself what it is that makes you thoughtful, and how you demonstrate this to other people in a way that is important to them.

## VALUES

Values are beliefs that become pillars of how you lead your life. What are your values relative to close friends and partners? Are they meeting your needs? Are you meeting theirs?

It is important to know your own values, what they mean, and why they are important to you. Values give an understanding of what is most important to you. You will explore this further in a little bit with a **Values Elicitation**. I highly recommend that couples do this exercise together to better understand how they may be connected or disconnected.

## JUDGMENTS

Before you answer this question about judgments, think for a moment about a few areas in which you are most critical of other people. Likewise, you can look at how you may favorably judge a person. Both might be inaccurate or be a small piece of the picture, however. Think of ways you might see someone favorably yet overlook their flaws, or primarily focus on someone's flaws and overlook their positives. Through years of observation and experience, you have generalized how you see or feel about groups of people. This is part of the normal role of the unconscious but is up to our conscious selves to be open to more possibilities.

## OBSTACLES

To be empowered you must be *At Cause* not *At Effect*. What that means is you must become a proactive go-getter of life and be your own cheerleader. You need to find ways to be in charge and not wait for things to happen. If that is how you are living most often, discover why. What are you afraid of? Why are you looking for obstacles to stop you rather than ways around them? If you find yourself waiting for the world to change for you, discover why. If you hear yourself making excuses about why something can't happen consider what it is you fear.

## ACCOUNTABILITY

When have you dropped the ball in your work or personal life and why did it happen? Maybe you just didn't care enough, were too mentally tired, or unaware. Ask yourself how you have been your own obstacle. Whatever it is, write it down in the exercise below. After you write those down, ask yourself if you need an accountability partner for some of these things.

As you do all the exercises know that they are a catalog of the real you, which allows you to be whole, honest, and consistent with your behaviors and actions.

## YOUR WHY

For any type of goal setting, you must have drivers and motivations behind them. Why are you doing the work? Ask yourself how your life is going to improve by becoming more aware and making positive changes.

# The Honesty Chart

<u>Instructions</u>

As you go through each area answer the questions with the first thought that comes to mind. That is your higher self, and it knows your real strengths and weaknesses. Your conscious mind keeps you from looking at what you don't want to see. It makes excuses and justifies your thoughts and behaviors.

**Once you are finished put this worksheet in a visible location so that you can refer to it daily as a reminder to stay focused on intentional living and enjoying your best, most fulfilled life.**

---

## SELF

List three favorable words that describe you. These words are what positively define <u>you and others would agree</u>. Go ahead and answer in the most honest way you can, even if it means skipping an adjective that you'd like to write down but know others would disagree.

1. ...................................... Why? ..............................................................................

2. ...................................... Why? ..............................................................................

3. ...................................... Why? ..............................................................................

List three negative words that describe you. Things you know you are but prefer not to admit.

1. ...................................... Why? ..............................................................................

2. ...................................... Why? ..............................................................................

3. ...................................... Why? ..............................................................................

---

9

## VALUES

List three words or short phrases that define your values and are essential in relationships with close friends and partners. Then, write down what that value means to you.

1. ............................ Means? ..................................................

....................................................................................

2. ............................ Means? ..................................................

....................................................................................

3. ............................ Means? ..................................................

....................................................................................

## JUDGMENTS

List three areas where you make judgments about others and create a person around them. (i.e., Parents who cuss a lot: Angry, thoughtless, uneducated. Overweight people: Sloppy, lazy, inactive. Valedictorian: Smart, driven, focused)

1. ............................ Describe ..................................................

....................................................................................

2. ............................ Describe ..................................................

....................................................................................

3. ............................ Describe ..................................................

....................................................................................

# OBSTACLES

First, pick one of the Sectors of Self:

Next, write down obstacles that have kept you from reaching a goal, a higher level of performance, or engaging in a relationship related to that Sector of Self.

Then, write down the alternative option that you could have done to work around that obstacle had you really set out to do it. Be honest, always be honest.

1. .......................... Alternative ....................................................................

2. .......................... Alternative ....................................................................

3. .......................... Alternative ....................................................................

# ACCOUNTABILITY

List three ways you have dropped the ball in work or your personal life. Why did it happen?

1. .......................... Why? ....................................................................

2. .......................... Why? ....................................................................

3. .......................... Why? ....................................................................

## What is my WHY?

I am going to expand my knowledge and awareness, have more self-love, better boundaries, more fulling and connected relationships, and a life filled with more purpose right now because:

.......................................................................................................................

.......................................................................................................................

.......................................................................................................................

# Sectors of Self

Instructions

Using Awareness & Accountability, score yourself in each of the Sectors of Self during the past six months based on the statements below.

|  | **Not at all** |  |  |  |  |  |  |  |  | **Definitely** |
|---|---|---|---|---|---|---|---|---|---|---|
| **Health & Fitness** | 1 | 2 | 3 | 4 | 5 | 6 | 7 | 8 | 9 | 10 |

I feel that my overall physical and emotional wellness is supporting my energy and motivation each day. I am rested and quiet-minded and can deal with life's challenges and opportunities. My food, activity, and sleep needs are a daily priority.

|  |  |  |  |  |  |  |  |  |  |  |
|---|---|---|---|---|---|---|---|---|---|---|
| **Relationships** | 1 | 2 | 3 | 4 | 5 | 6 | 7 | 8 | 9 | 10 |

I am deeply and lovingly connected to my partner. I am attentive and focused and make a true effort to spend quality time. I am patient, kind and listen to his/her needs, and communicate my own.

|  |  |  |  |  |  |  |  |  |  |  |
|---|---|---|---|---|---|---|---|---|---|---|
| **Friends & Family** | 1 | 2 | 3 | 4 | 5 | 6 | 7 | 8 | 9 | 10 |

I surround myself with people who enhance my life, love and support me. I recognize that I control who is in my immediate circle and that my own energy draws people into that circle. I am positive and authentic with the people closest to me.

| Personal Growth & Development | 1 | 2 | 3 | 4 | 5 | 6 | 7 | 8 | 9 | 10 |
|---|---|---|---|---|---|---|---|---|---|---|

I am always seeking ways to better myself, grow as a person, and inspire those around me. I have passion in my life be it through my career, hobbies, or regular activities. I believe my contribution to the world is valuable. I support and encourage those around me.

| Career & Finances | 1 | 2 | 3 | 4 | 5 | 6 | 7 | 8 | 9 | 10 |
|---|---|---|---|---|---|---|---|---|---|---|

I am excited and energized by my career and my contributions. I work to my best level and support my team as best I can. I am at the financial stage I currently desire and know there is financial abundance available should I seek more. I have a clear vision for career and lifestyle growth to best support me and my family and am on that path.

| Spirituality | 1 | 2 | 3 | 4 | 5 | 6 | 7 | 8 | 9 | 10 |
|---|---|---|---|---|---|---|---|---|---|---|

I feel connected to my higher self and the energies that surround me. I am content with my beliefs and behaviors, and my actions are rooted in the values that I hold.

Now, using your Sectors of Self exercise from above, I'd like you to take one of your lowest-scoring areas, one that if improved would cascade over into the other categories, and look at your values in that area. Values are deeply rooted beliefs that become a map of how to live your life and are stored in the unconscious mind. The unconscious acts as a tape looping in the background without your awareness and controls about 95% of your life. Anytime you are not fully present and conscious, your unconscious is at the helm.

Imagine for a moment that you scored a 5 in Career & Finances. You aren't earning enough, and keep getting passed over for promotions, new jobs, and so on. You want to earn more money. You need to earn more. Imagine you have already completed the upcoming Values Elicitation worksheet by writing down your values and realize that money didn't even make your values list.

There is nothing wrong with earning a well-paying living, and you may genuinely feel that way consciously. However, since the unconscious does not have "money" as a career value, you may find that situations and actions routinely play out to ensure that you are not meeting your earning potential. Deeper still, unconscious baggage (negative ideas or beliefs) about money will push you farther away from your income potential.

Unconscious baggage is what we uncover and eliminate during Mindset Transformation *Breakthrough Coaching*. Imagine for a moment you see a friend with her new designer handbag at the park and your first thought or comment is filled with contempt and sounds a little like, "Oh, she has to show off her new bag." That is baggage surrounding money and it's blocking your ability to earn more of it because of what wealth means to you at an unconscious level. Using this example, it seems like the unconscious views luxury goods as showing off, and there is likely a negative belief associated with money that limits earning potential.

# Values Elicitation

Set aside some time before you move into the next exercise. This is so important because it is another tool that requires time and insight so you can identify where conflicts lie. As a reminder, values are a word or short phrase that means something specific to you.

**Your homework is to select one of the Sectors of Self that needs your attention most, that if improved would create the greatest positive impact. You can, of course, do the following exercise with any sector.**

Please read the overview of instructions directly below. Afterward, you will have space to complete your Values Elicitation.

Instructions

1.  Begin by writing down things important to you in the selected Sector of Self.

For example, if you selected *Relationships* you might say "trust, fun, laughter, cooperation, shared interests."

*At some point, you are going to get stuck while coming up with words and phrases.*

2.  That's when you'll ask yourself, "If all those values existed what would make me leave my relationship?" You might say "infidelity," which means the opposite is a value to you, "fidelity."

3.  Then you would ask yourself, "If I had that whole list of values, and there was *infidelity*, what would make me stay in my relationship?" Perhaps therapy. But why? So, you can communicate and reconnect? This means "communication" and "connection" are also values.

**From my example, the list of Values in Relationships would look like this so far:**

**Trust, fun, laughter, cooperation, shared interests,**

plus, **fidelity, communication,** and **connection.**

This might open a mental block and you'll come up with several more words or phrases. For example, you may come up with new values like quality time, intimacy, and having children.

*Each time you get stuck you'll repeat 2 & 3 until you can't come up with anything else.*

- Once you have your word and phrase list eliminate the words that are different but have the same meaning, keeping the one that resonates best with you. For example, you might have written "sharing thoughts and feelings" and "communication" but have decided to include the phrase "quality communication" in your list to explain both.

- Then list your values in order of importance.

- Double-check that it all feels right and looks good to you then look at your Top 5. Those are *threshold* or *deal-breaker values*. If you are not getting those and you are still in your relationship, or at your job, for example, you probably feel unhappy inside. That is incongruency.

- Finally, write down what each value means to you.

Your values mean something different to you than they do to someone else. *Work/Life Balance* means something different to each person, *Fun* to one person might be partying on weekends, and to another, it might mean a nice dinner. For some the word *Healthy* might mean the ability to boulder and rock climb and to someone else it means good bloodwork.

Values are just labels. Understanding that opens your perspective and encourages you to ask more questions. I can't tell you how many times a day I ask, "When you say X, what does that mean?" so I am crystal clear about a person's thoughts and intentions. For example, "What do you mean when you say you want to relax this weekend?" or "You said you want to eat healthy, what does that look like to you?" Once you know someone better you might find yourself asking for fewer specifics because you have already learned about some of their values and meanings. However, if you are even a little bit uncertain, ask.

Select one of the Sectors of Self you need to work on right now, one where you want results or the area that when in better balance, would positively affect other areas of your life.

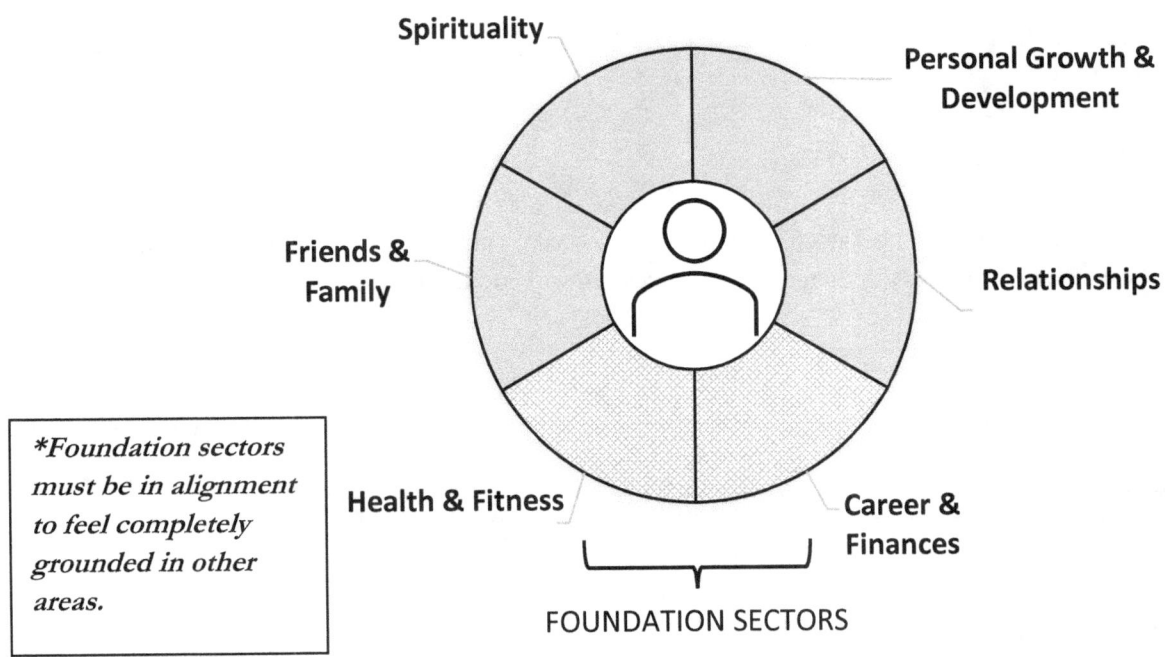

*Foundation sectors must be in alignment to feel completely grounded in other areas.*

FOUNDATION SECTORS

**Follow the prompts below to discover your values in the selected area and use the columns to write them down.**

1.  What is important to you about _____ (Sector of Self/area of life)?

    <u>Values List</u> (Brain dump three times to get as many initial words or phrases as you can.)

    _____     _____

    _____     _____

    _____     _____

    _____     _____

    _____     _____

    _____     _____

    _____     _____

2.  All these values being present, is there anything that could happen to make you leave/stop? (Write down the Value(s), which is the opposite. Consider the "infidelity/fidelity" example above.)

    _____     _____

    _____     _____

    _____     _____

3.  All these values being present, plus the Value(s) just mentioned, what would have to happen to make you stay/restart? (Write down the Value(s). Consider the therapy/communication and connection example above.)

    _____     _____

    _____     _____

    _____     _____

4. All these values being present, plus the Value(s) just mentioned, what would have to happen to make you leave/stop? (Write down the Value(s), which is the opposite. "Sudden illness" might make you stop something, so "being healthy" might be your value.)

_____     _____

_____     _____

_____     _____

- Continue with Steps 2 & 3 until you get repeat words, and add any new values that come to mind.

_____     _____

_____     _____

_____     _____

- Number the values according to their importance to you.

5. Rewrite the list of values according to their importance below.

   1. _____     6. _____

   2. _____     7. _____

   3. _____     8. _____

   4. _____     9. _____

   5. _____     10. _____

6.  Elicit the meaning for your Top 10.

When you say (Value), what does that mean to you?

<u>Value</u>                                    <u>Meaning</u>

*1. _____    _____

*2. _____    _____

*3. _____    _____

*4. _____    _____

*5. _____    _____

6. _____    _____

7. _____    _____

8. _____    _____

9. _____    _____

10. _____    _____

**\*Deal Breaker, or Threshold Values**

As I mentioned earlier, let's say you selected Career & Finances for your sector, and you say that money <u>and</u> flexibility are important values, but you are not achieving either. It is up to you to determine what personal baggage is in your way, how you can shift your perspective or environment, or evaluate if those values are your priorities or ones you think you *should* have.

Whether you are in a romantic relationship or working for a company, you are in a relationship. If you realize that you are often "battling" the other party, you can use a Values Elicitation to determine if your values overlap. This is especially useful in romantic relationships.

If long hours, understaffing, and infrequent raises are common practices in your company and you desire to work reasonably hard while having some flexibility with customary raises, it's clear you are going to be unhappy with your job. Likewise, if you have a romantic partner who enjoys fun, good communication, and being active, all things you like, too, but you are unsatisfied in your relationship, it's time to determine what those values mean to each of you.

As you become more accepting of your values and who you are, you will notice that how you show up will realign to reflect how you feel inside.

# TENET 2
# PSYCHOLOGICAL CONGRUENCE

---

**Themes:**

- Understanding the relationship of the Higher Self, Conscious Mind, and Unconscious Mind.
- Identifying how you describe yourself without judgment.
- Evaluating past and current situations when you did not follow your intuition.
- Learning to analyze thoughts and experiences and how you can reshape them.

**Exercise Topics:** *3-Self Conversation Conflict, Self-Talk, Decision Time, Shape Your Mind*

---

So far you have done exercises pertaining to Self, Values, Judgments, Obstacles, and Accountability, and had an honest opportunity to look inward. Remember, it's about learning, growing, and improving by way of personal insight, and by learning about other people's reality and where they might be coming from.

In this section of the workbook, you are going to look at the *3-Selves*, work through your *Self-Talk*, and discuss how to *Shape Your Mind* for a more productive and positive outlook. As you move forward, continue to do the companion exercises concurrently with your reading of "FEELING STUCK?" This will keep the information fresh in your mind and help you excel in your mindset transformation.

## 3-SELVES Review

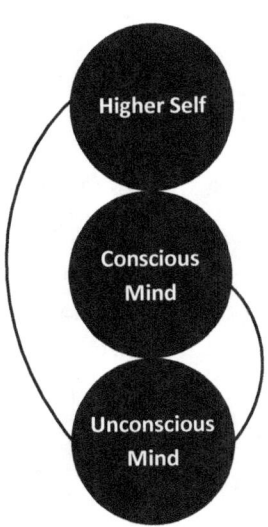

HS: Reminds you of who you are on a soul level and the lessons you need to learn.

CM: Reasoning that justifies actions and behaviors. Often hedonistic and seeking to please or protect us in the moment.

UM: One of the prime directives of the unconscious mind is protection — often burying negative emotions that are released when triggered.

The *Higher Self (HS)* reminds you of who you are and the lessons you need to learn. It's that part of you that says things like: "That's not who you are," or "You were meant for more." This is the highest, most spiritually connected level of "self" responsible for intuition or gut responses. It is also the level of "self" people are most often disconnected from.

The *Conscious Mind (CM)* is the very human part that can justify any thought or action, good or bad, based on the identity a person has of themselves. It is amazing at reasoning and can talk a person into or out of something.

The *Unconscious Mind (UM)* is the little voice that often conflicts with the reasoning of the conscious mind and puts baggage in the way of the higher self. It is what you truly believe and is hardwired from the values, beliefs, and experiences you have collected. The unconscious mind plays like a tape recorder in the background and takes over any time a person is not fully present or mindful. *The unconscious mind runs more than 95% of your life.*

# 3-SELF CONVERSATION CONFLICT

To help you become aware of any conflicts you have faced, I have given you examples of the 3-Self Conversation Conflict below. This exercise will help you see where your conflicts come from, while the **Decision Time Exercise** will help you work through them with *positive self-talk*.

---

*Example 1: You are considering moving in with a friend to save money so you can buy a home.*

CM (Thoughts): I don't want to move twice and put stuff in storage. The cat will be upset with a temporary move. I'll make do but be bothered because I really want to own rather than rent.

UM: It feels like a step backward in my life.

HS: You'll need to swallow your ego to move forward. This is your lesson for now.

** Incongruent. The UM is providing a roadblock and the CM is creating reasons to justify the UM.


*Example 2: A friend asked you for a favor and you felt bad saying "no."*

CM (Thoughts): I'm a terrible friend because I won't take her to the airport at 3 a.m.

UM: I'm selfish.

HS: No, you aren't a bad friend. You have boundaries and you will be a wreck tomorrow at work. She has other options like ride share and different friends to ask. Why does her preference to be driven override your need to be alert and functional the next day?

**Congruent. The HS and CM made the decision to not go despite the negative talk of the UM.

---

Let's look at *Example 1* more in-depth. First, know this is an actual summarized discussion with a good friend years ago. She wanted to buy a house but didn't have the down payment and was paying way too much for an apartment. One of her friends offered her a place to stay (for free!) for a few months so she could save up money for a down payment.

My friend intuitively knew that staying in the apartment was a waste of money and it was holding her back from saving for what she really wanted but kept giving herself surface, reasoned excuses as to why she should stay. (Like moving twice is a pain, the cat would be nervous, I don't want to impose, and so on.)

So, there we were, having this discussion about her conflict and I just stopped her at like excuse number six and said, *I'd like you to take a few breaths and quiet your mind, and I'm going to ask you a question. "Tell me the very first thing that comes to mind no matter what it is. 'Why don't you want to move into your friend's place?'"* And her response was *"It feels like a step backwards."*

Now that is honest, right? She was using so many limiting excuses because she unconsciously felt like it was a step backward. I reframed the scenario for her and asked her if our roles were reversed would she see my moving into the friend's home as a step backward? She said, no.

I asked her if she would feel imposed upon if she was the one offering space to a friend. Again, she said no. I also reminded her that moving to a temporary location would open energetic space for what she wanted. We also did the money savings math together.

But more than anything, she admitted the real, underlying excuse was her baggage. Once you allow the real reasons to appear you can address them and make clear-headed, cohesive movement toward what your unified self wants.

If you want to know how the story ends, she moved in with her friend a couple of weeks later, found a perfect home for herself in a few months, and had the down payment she needed. Plus, the friend got to have someone living in her house when she traveled. Everyone won!

Let's take a closer look at *Example 2* where there is congruence despite having negative self-talk. That person would have been okay with her decision to say "no" but to eliminate any doubt and feel at peace she would need to let go of her self-imposed conscious and unconscious verbal flogging.

She was able to override her negative self-talk to make the best decision for the scenario. Saying "no" and having boundaries is okay and is in alignment with the higher self and the decision. We'll discuss knowing and accepting boundaries more during the *6ᵗʰ Tenet of Mindset Transformation – Confidence & Boundaries*.

Using the same example, *if she had agreed* to take her friend, in order to be fully accepting of her choice, she would need to have made a clear-headed decision without guilt, and honor she was not going to get the rest she needed. This would allow her to move forward without resentment, bitterness, or the belief she could hold it over the friend's head as a favor card. Her higher self would have accepted it as a periodic sacrifice of inconvenience that people sometimes make. You always have a choice: Want to vs. Have to.

When you make choices that involve other people you must accept the reality of your choices without blaming or being a victim of them. They must be from your own emotionally-neutral free will. Likewise, it is the other person's responsibility to accept your choice as such. There is little worse than having someone apologize to you a dozen times for your helping them and explaining over and over that they feel bad. That is their baggage, and it is sure to land heavy on someone eventually.

Using the examples above, think of a conflicting scenario that has been pulling you back and forth about what decision is best. It might be a simple decision or one with more profound impact. Or, remember a time or two when you didn't do something because fear, an excuse, or a limiting belief held you back. Use your personal scenarios for the exercise below.

# 3-Self Conversation Conflict

Instructions

**To discover what your Unconscious Mind really feels, take a few filling breaths, quiet your mind, and ask the simple question of "why" or "why not" you want something. Listen to the first thought that comes to mind. It will require honesty, awareness, openness, and no judgment from you.**

CM: All the reasons you are justifying your decision.

UM: What the little voice said.

HS: The bigger picture, higher self lesson you can take from the experience.

*Scenario 1:* _____

CM (Thoughts): ....................................................................................................................

UM: ....................................................................................................................

HS ....................................................................................................................

*Scenario 2:* _____

CM (Thoughts): ....................................................................................................................

UM: ....................................................................................................................

HS ....................................................................................................................

*Scenario 3:* _____

CM (Thoughts): ....................................................................................................................

UM: ....................................................................................................................

HS ....................................................................................................................

As you begin to really listen to your language consider how you can reframe a "Nothing is ever easy" motto into a self-discovery lesson about why that feels true.

Are you an active participant in life or a passive one? Does life happen to you or are you being proactive in reshaping it? You are here so you must be somewhat proactive, right? I call that being *At Cause* or being empowered vs. *At Effect* which is a state of victimhood. If "Nothing is ever easy" feels true for you it is very likely that you are letting life happen *to you*. I have a good friend that jokes it is her family's motto. While I love them all as people, I can say that I have heard about a good quantity of decisions that went poorly due to lack of planning, research and proactivity.

Challenges in life are normal, in fact, they are required. Without them people often forget how completely capable and resourceful they can be. It's a muscle that must be flexed periodically to remind you of your abilities. It's no secret that people often get in their own way with negative self-talk and limiting beliefs about who they are and their abilities.

# Self-Talk

For the next exercise, I'm asking you to go inward and take an honest inventory of how you see yourself, how you believe others see you, and how your life would change with a shift in mindset.

Instructions

To help you explore your true self further and the language you use to describe yourself, I want you to **write down the first thing that comes to mind, no matter what. It does not matter if it is something you like or don't like.**

My physical, mental, and emotional limitations that I hyper-focus on are:

.................................................................................................................................................

.................................................................................................................................................

.................................................................................................................................................

I think other people focus on these physical, mental, and emotional limitations about me:

.................................................................................................................................................

.................................................................................................................................................

.................................................................................................................................................

I am a great person because of these top 5 strengths:

My limitations and strengths conflict with each other in this way:

**Use a sticky note, a phone reminder, or whatever works best for you so you can see the following positive reminders throughout the day.**

If I focused on my strengths more than my limitations my life would change like this:

The part of my mindset that makes me successful is:

I will do this every day to remind myself of my strengths:

No matter what you believe to be true about yourself, the reality is that there are places where you are better, and other areas where you need improvement.

Maybe you wrote 'tenacious' as one of your strengths, how awesome! But maybe you also wrote 'stubborn' as a weakness. You won't ask for help or seek other options, so you often feel stuck or overwhelmed. If you wrote both "tenacious" and "stubborn" for example, you get the chance to determine if you are tenacious because you are stubborn, or vice versa. They are not synonyms. Imagine how effective tenacity is when you can forecast and know when and how to ask for help.

A head chef is more effective with a sous chef assisting, even if she can do it all. Just as I am capable of opening my own door but am happy to have a man or woman hold it for me as I enter. I do the same for them. My refusal to have someone hold my door might mean I feel weak or subordinate, or that I believe they see me as incapable. In my case as a woman, I have heard various men throughout my life refuse to let me hold a door for them, often citing a value surrounding gender roles.

Ask yourself what you need to <u>not believe</u> about asking for help or planning better that would allow you to be less stubborn. That is when you will learn about your unconscious baggage.

Now, let's look at some decisions you may have made recently that didn't feel good, and current situations where you might be feeling the common inner conflict of "I need to do this but want to do that." The reason for these exercises is to give you the space and room to freely allow whatever comes to mind. There are no wrong or right answers. Give yourself the space and freedom to accept whatever comes up.

# Decision Time

<u>Instructions</u>

**Think about two recent decisions which didn't feel like the right choice intuitively. Write down the decisions you made, and the instinct your unconscious mind told you to make but you did not choose.**

To be clear, I am looking for examples where <u>you chose to do something that didn't feel right but you did it anyway.</u> This is totally different than the inner battle I imagine you've had where the choice you made was difficult on the surface, but you felt like you followed your gut. Relationships are a good example, romantic or friend. For as difficult as it may have been to cut ties with your friend of many years because you knew it would end your hanging out with a certain friend group, you did it anyway because inside you also knew that letting go of the toxic energy would open space for positive energy and long-term growth. Now that is tough and an awesome choice. So that is <u>not</u> the example we want.

**Two recent decisions I made which didn't feel like the right choice intuitively, and the choice my instincts told me to make but I didn't choose.**

1. Situation .......................... Decision I did not make despite my intuition

2. Situation .......................... Decision I did not make despite my intuition

Now, think of times when <u>you didn't do something</u> because fear, an excuse, or a limiting belief held you back. Then uncover the limiting belief holding you back using your tools from the *3-Self Conversation Conflict*.

**Three situations I am <u>currently</u> faced with that sound something like "I know I should do *this,* but I have to do *that* instead." (i.e., "I should leave my spouse because our relationship is toxic, but I don't know if I am ready to be a single parent," or "I need to finish my education to have a better long-term career, but I have to keep doing this dead-end job because I need the money right now.")**

*Situation*                                      *Reason I Should...*

**Ex. Divorcing spouse**                  **Unhealthy relationship, and bad for the kids to see.**

**Limiting belief(s) holding me back:** <u>I never thought I would divorce, and it feels like failing, people will think I am selfish for leaving, and I don't know if I am capable of parenting mostly alone.</u>

*Situation*                                      *Reason I Should...*

**Ex. Pursuing education**                **More career opportunities when I finish.**

**Limiting belief(s) holding me back:** <u>What if getting more education doesn't help me, I don't know if I can sustain school and work at least part-time, and I don't think I have a support system.</u>

1. Situation .................... Reason I Should ....................

............................................................................

**Limiting belief(s) holding me back: ....................................

............................................................................

............................................................................

2. Situation .................... Reason I Should ....................

............................................................................

**Limiting belief(s) holding me back: ....................................

............................................................................

............................................................................

3. Situation .................... Reason I Should ....................

............................................................................

**Limiting belief(s) holding me back: ....................................

............................................................................

Just as you learned earlier, once you determine the inner conflict keeping you from making a good decision, even if difficult, you will be better able to make tough choices moving forward. In fact, the more experience you have staying **psychologically congruent** the easier it will be to live a more peaceful life. Life fulfillment is possible when coupled with an honest acceptance of personal values, quality communication, empathy, and boundaries.

# Shape Your Mind

Instructions

Think about times when you have made choices to disconnect, become negatively triggered, or have felt lost or alone. Consider times in your life that you know the outcome could have been different because of hindsight or through observation. Select any area of life that feels right to you.

Positive mind shaping requires empowered thinking about where you have more and less control, and how you can choose to respond differently to a situation.

# Part 1

### Example

When I (feel/act) _like no one cares about me because they don't invite me to the movies_, I will choose to be open-minded and (feel/do) _reach out to someone and invite them to go, knowing they might not be able to this time_ instead.

When I (feel/act) _sulk because I feel like I will never be promoted at work because I don't have the same experience as others_, I will choose to be open-minded and (feel/do) _realize that everyone started somewhere, then ask my boss for guidance about what I need to do in order to keep growing at work_ instead.

When I (feel/act) ............................................................................................................... ,

I will choose to be open-minded and (feel/do) ...........................................................................

............................................................................................................................... instead.

When I (feel/act) ............................................................................................................... ,

I will choose to be open-minded and (feel/do) ...........................................................................

............................................................................................................................... instead.

When I (feel/act) ............................................................................................................... ,

I will choose to be open-minded and (feel/do) ...........................................................................

............................................................................................................................... instead.

You get to decide how your life will unfold at any time and know that how you feel is often your interpretation. Every scenario is different. A new perspective often helps mitigate a negative response. I challenge you to flip the scenario when you feel like something is happening to you and see if your perspective changes. Remember, no one thinks, feels nor observes the same things.

Rather than choose to be angry you didn't get a promotion like a co-worker, consider what he did to stand out. Did he often show how great he was doing or stay eager and engaged in meetings? Were you just sitting back waiting to be noticed because that's how you think it should be?

## The most successful people know how and when to adapt to their environment.

You will always have challenges. Learning to pause and calmly assess, so you can determine how to move through, around, or from those challenges is what you need to be empowered in your life.

Instructions

Take a few deep breaths and quiet your mind, knowing anything that comes up is okay for your responses below. **Use whatever tools work best for you to remind yourself daily how you can reshape your mindset.**

## Part 2

Examples of when I have personalized a situation that I know was not really about me are:

The areas in my life where I feel the least control are:

I can reshape some aspects of those areas by:

Instead of allowing negative impulses to direct me, I will shift my thoughts and emotional energy towards the positive alternative by:

The happiest, most joyous people know that they are in control of their life outcome, and focus on positive thought patterns, behaviors, and actions to create the life they desire.

# TENET 3
# FOCUS

**Themes:**

- Helping you to identify topics of most importance and which ones to let go of for now.
- Identifying what pulls you away or distracts you when focusing on a specific item.
- Gaining clarity about your organization style and what will improve your focus and productivity.

**Exercise Topics:** *Clarity Assessment, Distraction Awareness, Organization & Attention*

The Thought and Emotion Value Scale (TEVS) helps assign value and/or emotion to any given thought (importance to remember, forget, act upon or not) and how long you want to focus on that thought.

Use TEVS to stay focused, prioritizing realistic goals and projects. The assessment below will help you establish focused commitments for the items you are most eager for. By focusing on what is most important and putting back-of-mind projects or goals on hold you will keep moving priority items forward with more focus and clarity.

# Clarity Assessment

Instructions

Describe in your mind a current project or goal. Rank its necessity and importance from 1 to 5. Be sure to notice what you write down and if they are ranked appropriately from a thought, emotion, and time commitment perspective. Each person will have his own perspective.

**Example**

*Project:_____Clean out the garage_____*

| TEVS Score | Interested but doesn't move me | | | Very excited and making progress | |
|---|---|---|---|---|---|
| | 1 | 2 | 3 | 4 | 5 |

❖ This project is important because:

*The garage clutter is making me crazy, and I can't find anything. Clutter is spilling into the house because I can't access what I need easily.*

❖ I will need to make these items a priority to make it happen:

*Buying a garage organization unit and bins for inside the unit, plus large stacking bins and trash bags.*

❖   I will schedule time (daily/weekly) as follows to make this project a reality:

*Begin throwing out and sorting what I keep on Sat & Sun AM for two hours each. Sort what will go in the storage unit and what will be stacked in large bins.*

---

*Project 1:* _____

**TEVS Score**   **Interested but doesn't move me**        **Very excited and making progress**

| 1 | 2 | 3 | 4 | 5 |

This project is important because:

I will need to make these items a priority to make it happen:

I will schedule time (daily/weekly) as follows to make this project a reality:

---

*Project 2:* _____

| TEVS Score | Interested but doesn't move me | | | Very excited and making progress | |
|---|---|---|---|---|---|
| | **1** | **2** | **3** | **4** | **5** |

This project is important because: .........................................................................................

..........................................................................................................................................

..........................................................................................................................................

..........................................................................................................................................

I will need to make these items a priority to make it happen: .......................................

..........................................................................................................................................

..........................................................................................................................................

I will schedule time (daily/weekly) as follows to make this project a reality: ...............

..........................................................................................................................................

..........................................................................................................................................

..........................................................................................................................................

*Project 3:* _____

| TEVS Score | Interested but doesn't move me | | | Very excited and making progress | |
|---|---|---|---|---|---|
| | 1 | 2 | 3 | 4 | 5 |

This project is important because: ....................................................................................

..........................................................................................................................

..........................................................................................................................

..........................................................................................................................

I will need to make these items a priority to make it happen: ........................................

..........................................................................................................................

..........................................................................................................................

..........................................................................................................................

I will schedule time (daily/weekly) as follows to make this project a reality: ...................

..........................................................................................................................

..........................................................................................................................

TEVS is not only great for helping you prioritize larger projects, but also a readiness scale. If you do not have the emotional bandwidth or genuine time to commit to something lingering in your mind, let it go for now. In order to be most productive, you must have a focused commitment on what you want to achieve now rather than overcommitting and underperforming or burning out.

Have you been focusing too much on items you ranked at a 3 or less? If so, you are likely to start movement on those projects but get lost or stuck then watch them fall away. At least for a while.

Have you ranked everything a 3 or less? If that is the case, it sounds like you have many agenda items that you believe you *should* do but are not committed to them. Evaluate whether those items are really of interest to you or someone else, and your readiness to tackle them. If it is not important to you right now let it go and preserve your mental and emotional energy for the areas you can be most productive.

Skip any project scoring less than a 3, for now.

To have optimal focus on what you want to achieve you must be aware of the people and things that distract you from the tasks you need to accomplish and the goals you have. Use this worksheet to help you identify when you are most distracted, by what, and an alternate solution.

# Distraction Awareness

Instructions

Rank each item's ability to cause you to stop or delay what you are doing. **Re-evaluate in one month.**

|  | Not at all |  |  |  | Definitely |
|---|---|---|---|---|---|
| Phone call (unknown caller) | 1 | 2 | 3 | 4 | 5 |
| Phone call (co-worker) | 1 | 2 | 3 | 4 | 5 |
| Phone call (family, non-emergency) | 1 | 2 | 3 | 4 | 5 |
| Smartwatch wrist vibration | 1 | 2 | 3 | 4 | 5 |
| Email or Text | 1 | 2 | 3 | 4 | 5 |
| Looking up something not related to the moment | 1 | 2 | 3 | 4 | 5 |
| Laundry | 1 | 2 | 3 | 4 | 5 |
| Another task on your list | 1 | 2 | 3 | 4 | 5 |
| Something else you suddenly decided to do | 1 | 2 | 3 | 4 | 5 |
| Non-urgent needs of other people nearby | 1 | 2 | 3 | 4 | 5 |

*Re-prioritize distractions you rank 3 or more.*

Allocate chunks of time with **Time Blocking** for anything ranked 3 or more because those items are most distracting and steal your focus and productivity. You can use your hourly break to address texts and emails, or phone calls, for example, rather than responding in the moment to each one. This tactic allows you to stay focused on what you are doing, knowing you will move through the distraction items as a collective during a designated time block.

Who among us has not been pulled away by a sudden thought and found themself doing something totally different? Imagine you are in a groove at work when a colleague says something that piques your interest and bam, you are suddenly lost in a super sleuth research project. The groove you had going on the work-specific project you had is gone. Or you are home doing regular house cleaning and see a dirty baseboard, then moments later, in the middle of vacuuming, you are touching it up with paint you had to dig out from some buried location.

Use your **Waitlist** for impulse control items. This is where you jot down a quick note of what you suddenly wanted to look up or a non-urgent task that just popped into your mind that you instantly want to address. Address those topics during one of your breaks or create a specific **Time Block** for it.

---

As you consider the questions below, ask yourself **why** you answered the way you did. What aspects of your environment or energy, for example, keep you distracted or focused?

I find myself most distracted when I am:

........................................................................................

........................................................................................

........................................................................................

The times of day I feel least focused are:

........................................................................................

........................................................................................

........................................................................................

The times of day I feel most focused are:

........................................................................................

........................................................................................

........................................................................................

I can use Time Blocking to chunk together these areas of distraction:

........................................................................................

........................................................................................

........................................................................................

I can improve my focus at work by:

........................................................................................

........................................................................................

........................................................................................

I can improve my focus at home by: ...........................................................................................................

.....................................................................................................................................................

.....................................................................................................................................................

I can improve my mental clarity with food and water by: ...............................................................

.....................................................................................................................................................

.....................................................................................................................................................

Remember, you must STOP and START things to be most effective. Awareness and management of distractions are necessary to become more organized. Like with anything, you must evaluate where you are most successful and thriving, and where you are dropping the ball when it comes to organization.

# Organization & Attention

## Part 1

<u>Instructions</u>

Rank each item as you are today. **Re-evaluate in one month.**

|  | Never |  |  |  | Always |
|---|---|---|---|---|---|
| I write a task list | 1 | 2 | 3 | 4 | 5 |
| I set reminders on my digital calendar | 1 | 2 | 3 | 4 | 5 |
| I add appointments to my digital calendar | 1 | 2 | 3 | 4 | 5 |
| I prioritize what I need to accomplish each day | 1 | 2 | 3 | 4 | 5 |
| I schedule time for me | 1 | 2 | 3 | 4 | 5 |
| I create realistic time blocks to accomplish each task | 1 | 2 | 3 | 4 | 5 |
| I designate specific locations to do some things | 1 | 2 | 3 | 4 | 5 |
| I get up and move for a few minutes each hour | 1 | 2 | 3 | 4 | 5 |

*Start doing anything you ranked less than a 3.*

## Part 2

|  | Never |  |  | Always |
|---|---|---|---|---|
| I do things as I remember them regardless of importance | 1 | 2 | 3 | 4 |
| Even if I can't keep my eyes open, I push on | 1 | 2 | 3 | 4 |
| I jump from one item to the next, rarely completing a single item efficiently | 1 | 2 | 3 | 4 |
| I let the day happen *to me* | 1 | 2 | 3 | 4 |

*Modify your behavior so your score becomes 2 or less.*

Distractions are what need to be stopped while organization is what needs to start. Even without distractions, you will find yourself stuck if you have no plan. In Part One above, you looked at the tools you are using to stay focused and on-task, and considered if where and when you are doing specific items is maximizing your time. You might use tools not listed. Whatever you are using, if it works, keep doing it.

Everyone has a different organization method that works for them even within the boundaries of the same tool. Let's look at **Task Lists.** Sounds simple but for you that might mean:

- Sticky notes everywhere
- For another person, it might be a single list on a notepad that gets checked off as it is completed.
- Someone else might use an app or calendar reminder and task lists on their mobile device or computer.

You must find what works for you. I have found that for my clients, Task Lists in some form are great for simple items and give a sense of accomplishment as each item gets checked off. The more accomplished you feel the more inspired you are to keep moving.

By now you should be getting into a habit of taking hourly breaks to refocus and re-energize and do positive things for you. This might be simple stretching or refueling with a snack or water. Never underestimate the importance of food and water to keep you functioning at your optimum.

The second part of this exercise discussed how proactive you are in your day. You get to choose how you manage what pops into your mind and take control of when you address everything. In "FEELING STUCK?," you also learned about the importance of rest. Without proper rest, it is difficult to remain alert throughout the day. Ever read something over and over for thirty minutes and still have no idea what you read because you were so tired? Learning to nap, meditate or use hypnosis for twenty to thirty minutes will transform your focus and clarity. The challenge I have found with most clients is that they think they need to power through, believing that the time they are taking to recharge will take away from productivity. In fact, the opposite is true.

**To focus so you can be more productive you must:**

- Become aware of and manage distractions.
- Get rid of tasks or projects that are not meaningful, or you do not have time for so your energy is available for areas you can focus on and complete.
- Learn how to organize your time efficiently.

# TENET 4
# PRODUCTIVITY

---

**Themes:**

- The first step of goal setting is knowing what outcomes you want to achieve.
- Identifying important projects, forecasting needs, and prioritizing tasks and people needed to accomplish a goal.
- Organizing individual components of a larger project, or one-off tasks that you need to complete.

**Exercise Topics:** *Goal Setting, Project Planner, Task Planner, Time Blocking*

---

Goal setting is energetic direction. It's like giving lightning a place to strike. Electrical energy in the cloud strikes with electrons on the ground. The ground tells the lightning where to strike. Without an idea or thought, kind of like the electrons on the ground, you are not giving yourself a direction for your energy and actions. You need something to connect with to stay goal focused.

# Goal Setting

<u>Instructions</u>

For each goal, identify how it will benefit you and what you will need to make it a reality.

Use this tool for *Professional* long-term and short-term goals, *Personal* long-term and short-term goals, and any upcoming projects.

**Professional Examples:** Find a new job, learn a new skill, become more focused, and create better work/life boundaries.

**Personal Examples:** Plan a vacation, find a new hobby, focus on wellness, and connect with more people.

**Project Examples:** Buy a new home/car, home remodel.

**Goal 1:** _____

This goal is relevant now or to my future self because:

I would be passionate and proud to do this because:

How I can accomplish this goal without sacrificing too much time, energy, money, or other resources needed elsewhere:

A realistic time frame needed to accomplish this goal is:

The resources I will need, other than myself, to make this happen are:

I have the support of the following people around me:

The people and obstacles that might stand in my way of reaching this goal are:

If this goal is to become a reality, I will need to shift my life priorities by:

I am going to dedicate this specific time to my goal (daily time block or weeks/months depending on type):

**Goal 2:** _____

This goal is relevant now or to my future self because:

I would be passionate and proud to do this because:

How I can accomplish this goal without sacrificing too much time, energy, money, or other resources needed elsewhere:

A realistic time frame needed to accomplish this goal is:

The resources I will need, other than myself, to make this happen are:

I have the support of the following people around me: ..........................................................

..........................................................................................................................................

..........................................................................................................................................

The people and obstacles that might stand in my way of reaching this goal are: ........................

..........................................................................................................................................

..........................................................................................................................................

If this goal is to become a reality, I will need to shift my life priorities by: ...............................

..........................................................................................................................................

..........................................................................................................................................

I am going to dedicate this specific time to my goal (daily time block or weeks/months depending on type):

..........................................................................................................................................

..........................................................................................................................................

# Project Planner

Instructions

The Project Planner will help you block time and organize your current projects.

**Project:** _____     **Due Date:** _____

**Phase 1.** First 5 items I need to move forward.     **Phase 2.** Next 5 items I need to move forward.

1. _____     1. _____

2. _____     2. _____

3. _____     3. _____

4. _____     4. _____

5. _____     5. _____

**PRIORITY TASKS – These must be finished before moving on to anything or anyone else TODAY.**

1. _____     3. _____

2. _____     4. _____

**PEOPLE**

I MUST contact these people TODAY.     I'm waiting for information from these people. (With a planned follow-up date).

1. _____     1. _____ Date: _____

2. _____     2. _____ Date: _____

3. _____     3. _____ Date: _____

# Task Planner

Creating an overview and a plan are essential components of productivity – be it little tasks or bigger projects. The Task Planner is a simple checklist for individual tasks, or those from a larger project.

Instructions

Create a list that you can check off item by item to give yourself forward movement and a sense of accomplishment. You can create a digital version of this as well if it suits you best. There are also many Task List apps available.

**Must Do Today**

Item                                                    Notes

☐ _____    _____

☐ _____    _____

☐ _____    _____

☐ _____    _____

☐ _____    _____

☐ _____    _____

☐ _____    _____

**This Week**

☐ _____    _____

☐ _____    _____

☐ _____    _____

☐ _____    _____

☐ _____    _____

☐ _____    _____

☐ _____    _____

# Time Blocking

<u>Instructions</u>

Identity time requirements for each item from your task list as well as life activities such as grocery shopping.

Giving yourself a realistic timeframe will allow you to allocate time better and be more productive.

**Item**                                          **Time Requirement**

1. _____   Min/Hours: _____

2. _____   Min/Hours: _____

3. _____   Min/Hours: _____

4. _____   Min/Hours: _____

5. _____   Min/Hours: _____

# PRESENCE

## Themes:

- Learning how to let go of what is holding you back and becoming goal-directed.
- Creating small, actionable steps to keep you moving forward.

**Exercise Topics:** *Presence Evaluation, S.M.A.R.T. Goals*

# Presence Evaluation

Instructions

Using Awareness & Accountability, score yourself in each of the Sectors of Self <u>as of today</u> based on the statement, and answer the questions to help determine your current level of presence and how you can maximize it.

<u>Not at all</u>                                                    <u>Definitely</u>

**Health & Fitness**          1    2    3    4    5    6    7    8    9    10

I feel that my overall physical and emotional wellness is supporting my energy and motivation each day. I am rested and quiet-minded and can deal with life's challenges and opportunities. My food, activity, and sleep needs are a daily priority.

I manage my wellness as follows: ...........................................................................................

...........................................................................................

...........................................................................................

...........................................................................................

I would be healthier if I was more proactive and did the following: .............................................

...........................................................................................

...........................................................................................

| **Relationships** | 1 | 2 | 3 | 4 | 5 | 6 | 7 | 8 | 9 | 10 |
|---|---|---|---|---|---|---|---|---|---|---|

I am deeply and lovingly connected to my partner. I am attentive and focused and make a true effort to spend quality time. I am patient, kind and listen to his/her needs, and communicate my own.

When I am with my partner I am usually (i.e., actively engaged, doing work, playing video games, texting):

.................................................................................................................

.................................................................................................................

.................................................................................................................

I know my partner would like it if we were more (i.e., connected, happy, secure) _____ and I can do the following to help ensure that happens from my side, knowing I am only responsible for me:

.................................................................................................................

.................................................................................................................

.................................................................................................................

| **Friends & Family** | 1 | 2 | 3 | 4 | 5 | 6 | 7 | 8 | 9 | 10 |
|---|---|---|---|---|---|---|---|---|---|---|

I surround myself with people who enhance my life, love and support me. I recognize that I control who is in my immediate circle and that my own energy draws people into that circle. I am positive and authentic with the people closest to me.

I engage with family and friends in the following ways: ...............................................

.................................................................................................................

.................................................................................................................

I will initiate the following to further connect on a weekly basis (i.e., invite to dinner, catch up on the phone, go to a community event): ...............................................

.................................................................................................................

.................................................................................................................

| Personal Growth & Development | 1 | 2 | 3 | 4 | 5 | 6 | 7 | 8 | 9 | 10 |
|---|---|---|---|---|---|---|---|---|---|---|

I am always seeking ways to better myself, grow as a person, and inspire those around me. I have passion in my life be it through my career, hobbies, or regular activities. I believe my contribution to the world is valuable. I support and encourage those around me.

The time I spend focusing on my personal growth looks like:

......................................................................................................................................

......................................................................................................................................

......................................................................................................................................

I can further enrich myself by (i.e., reading, volunteering, learning a skill):

......................................................................................................................................

......................................................................................................................................

......................................................................................................................................

| Career & Finances | 1 | 2 | 3 | 4 | 5 | 6 | 7 | 8 | 9 | 10 |
|---|---|---|---|---|---|---|---|---|---|---|

I am excited and energized by my career and my contributions. I work to my best level and support my team as best I can. I am at the financial stage I currently desire and know there is financial abundance available should I seek more. I have a clear vision for career and lifestyle growth to best support me and my family and am on that path.

When I think about my career and finances, I would describe my approach toward growth as:

......................................................................................................................................

......................................................................................................................................

......................................................................................................................................

If I implement the following, I will be more excited about and focused during each day, as well as the next step in my career:

......................................................................................................................................

......................................................................................................................................

......................................................................................................................................

| **Spirituality** | 1 | 2 | 3 | 4 | 5 | 6 | 7 | 8 | 9 | 10 |
|---|---|---|---|---|---|---|---|---|---|---|

I feel connected to my higher self and the energies that surround me. I am content with my beliefs and behaviors, and my actions are rooted in the values that I hold.

I do the following to make time for my spiritual and/or mind-quieting practice: ..........................................

.....................................................................................................................................................

.....................................................................................................................................................

.....................................................................................................................................................

I know my (i.e., anxiety, trust, patience) _____ would improve if I spent more time

incorporating the following into each day: ..........................................................................................

.....................................................................................................................................................

.....................................................................................................................................................

Now that you have scored yourself in each of the Sectors of Self. How did you do? **Go ahead and total up all the numbers, and flag anything under an 8.**

If you did not end up with a score of 48 or more, then it's likely you have been out of balance or fallen off your game recently, or perhaps you are realizing the areas you have often neglected. If you didn't score at least 48, that's okay because those numbers under 8 are just showing you where you need to focus attention. If the **career & finances** or **health & wellness** sectors fall under that mark, then definitely focus there since they are foundation sectors of self.

For the sectors you scored less than an 8, ask yourself what behavior you could begin in order to increase the score, or what limiting belief you need to stop to make room for improvement. If you scored 8 or above in any area, think about the difference that made the difference. Why is it you scored so much higher in that area? Consider how you can apply any positive momentum or lessons to the lower-scored areas to lift those scores as well.

During the Tenet 1 of this companion workbook to "FEELING STUCK?" you rated yourself in each of the Sectors of Self. Compare your scores above to Tenet 1 to help determine in what areas you need to continue to place more focus. Do this as needed to keep yourself moving forward.

| | Tenet 1 | Today | _____ | _____ | _____ |
|---|---|---|---|---|---|
| **Health & Fitness** | | | | | |
| **Relationships** | | | | | |
| **Friends & Family** | | | | | |
| **Personal Growth & Development** | | | | | |
| **Career & Finances** | | | | | |
| **Spirituality** | | | | | |
| **TOTAL** | | | | | |

# S.M.A.R.T. Goal Setting

Instructions

Use the following guidelines to establish achievable goals for each of the Sectors of Self, *ensuring that your motivation utilizes a proactive Towards strategy.*

**S – Specific/Simple**

**M – Measurable/Meaningful to You**

**A – Achievable/As if Now**

**R – Realistic/Responsible**

**T – Timed/Toward Your Goal**

## Motivation Strategies — 2 Types

**Towards:** My goal is to feel better and better.

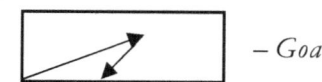 *+ Goal*

**Away From:** I'm motivated to not feel XYZ, but as I feel better, I fall off.

*– Goal*

### Friends Example

**Goal:** To reconnect with people and become more social by reaching out more.

**S(pecific/Simple)** – Call or text one person per week to set up one social engagement per month.

**M(eaningful/Measurable)** – Re-engagement with people so I feel less lonely.

**A(chievable/As if Now)** – I used to be more social and enjoyed it, and know others feel similar.

**R(ealisitic/Responsible)** – I can plan at least one social event without feeling overwhelmed.

**T(imed/Towards Goal)** – Per week/month basis to create social engagement I want.

[Small, positive steps directed *towards* a monthly socialization goal.]

| **Health & Fitness** |
| --- |
| **Goal:** _____ |
| **S(pecific/Simple)** – |
| **M(eaningful/Measurable)** – |
| **A(chievable/As if Now)** – |
| **R(ealisitic/Responsible)** – |
| **T(imed/Towards Goal)** – |

## Relationships

Goal: _____

**S(pecific/Simple)** –

**M(eaningful/Measurable)** –

**A(chievable/As if Now)** –

**R(ealisitic/Responsible)** –

**T(imed/Towards Goal)** –

## Friends & Family

Goal: _____

**S(pecific/Simple)** –

**M(eaningful/Measurable)** –

**A(chievable/As if Now)** –

**R(ealisitic/Responsible)** –

**T(imed/Towards Goal)** –

<u>**Personal Growth & Development**</u>

**Goal:** _____

**S**(pecific/Simple) – ...............................................................................................................................

........................................................................................................................................................

**M**(eaningful/Measurable) – .......................................................................................................

........................................................................................................................................................

**A**(chievable/As if Now) – ...........................................................................................................

........................................................................................................................................................

**R**(ealisitic/Responsible) – .........................................................................................................

........................................................................................................................................................

**T**(imed/Towards Goal) – .............................................................................................................

........................................................................................................................................................

<u>**Career & Finances**</u>

**Goal:** _____

**S**(pecific/Simple) – ...............................................................................................................................

........................................................................................................................................................

**M**(eaningful/Measurable) – .......................................................................................................

........................................................................................................................................................

**A**(chievable/As if Now) – ...........................................................................................................

........................................................................................................................................................

**R**(ealisitic/Responsible) – .........................................................................................................

........................................................................................................................................................

**T**(imed/Towards Goal) – .............................................................................................................

........................................................................................................................................................

**Spirituality**

Goal: _____

S(pecific/Simple) –

M(eaningful/Measurable) –

A(chievable/As if Now) –

R(ealisitic/Responsible) –

T(imed/Towards Goal) –

Once you have created your S.M.A.R.T. Goals, determine a plan of action to achieve each step. Stay focused and flexible with an unwavering commitment to reaching your goal. If something doesn't work, try something else. If you find something that is very effective, keep doing more of the same. Find role models and tools that have proven their effectiveness and be open to modifying wherever you may need to, if necessary.

If something has shown itself to be effective believe it. Too often, people modify a process or technique before trying it. This is very common in business when a new policy is implemented, and people automatically declare why it won't work as described or at all for their department or store before trying it. Get out of your own way, let go of being stubborn and be present, truly focusing on what you need to do and giving it a fair shot. You can always modify it moving forward.

# TENET 6
## CONFIDENCE & BOUNDARIES

---

**Themes:**

- Assessing your upbringing and belief system.
- Learning how to define, create, and uphold your boundaries while respecting those of others.

**Exercise Topics:** *Confidence & Boundary Assessment, Boundary Setting*

---

# Confidence & Boundary Assessment

Developing confidence begins at the earliest stages of human development. With confidence comes your ability to establish and respect boundaries. Please answer the questions below to gain further insight about yourself.

**Please rank your experience from 1 (least agreement) to 5 (most agreement) in each of the boxes.**

1.  My caregivers/teachers minimized moments that filled me with pride or excitement. ☐

Explain:

.................................................................................................................................

.................................................................................................................................

.................................................................................................................................

2.  I grew up in an environment where most things were done for me (i.e., cleaning my room, cooking, being woken up for school, parental intervention instead of speaking for myself...). ☐

Explain:

.................................................................................................................................

.................................................................................................................................

.................................................................................................................................

3. I am worried about not fitting into cultural norms. ☐

Explain:

_____

_____

4. My self-criticism or my perceived judgments by other people holds me back. ☐

Explain:

_____

_____

5. I am not complete unless I have a companion. ☐

Explain:

_____

_____

6. I am not good enough no matter how successful I become or what I accomplish. ☐

Explain:

_____

_____

Observe which statements above you ranked higher than 3. These are areas that are **holding you back** from mastering personal fulfillment. Once you recognize your inherent self-bias, judgments, and insecurities you can improve upon them when ready. For many people, Mindset Transformation Coaching® on its own will help transform those areas that need the most help, while others may require talk therapy or massive action like environmental changes to leap beyond their perceived limitations.

If you consistently ranked yourself less than a 3, congratulations. You likely had a childhood that helped develop your belief in yourself and recognize your abilities. If you didn't or it was so-so, you are doing a great job of honoring your abilities, worth and growth potential as an individual today.

**Please rank your experience from 1 (least agreement) to 5 (most agreement) in each of the boxes.**

1.  I recognize how personal insecurity is transmitted via behavior in all types of relationships, and that I am responsible for what I transmit and aware of what I am receiving. ☐

Explain: ......................................................................................................................................

......................................................................................................................................

......................................................................................................................................

2.  I was given room to learn/explore on my own as a young child and through my teenage years. ☐

Explain: ......................................................................................................................................

......................................................................................................................................

......................................................................................................................................

3.  I am a person of good quality and character. ☐

Explain: ......................................................................................................................................

......................................................................................................................................

......................................................................................................................................

4.  I enjoy trying new things and don't compare myself to others. ☐

Explain: ......................................................................................................................................

......................................................................................................................................

......................................................................................................................................

5.  I realize that when I am trying to grow as a person, there are other people who have had a head start. I use those people to model their success rather than compare my novice level to their expert level. ☐

Explain: ......................................................................................................................................

......................................................................................................................................

......................................................................................................................................

6. I believe that I have a great capacity for growth. ☐

Explain:

7. My needs and values are my own. I am not bound to the values I learned from caretakers when I was a child. ☐

Explain:

8. I give room for friends and family to freely express their needs and boundaries. ☐

Explain:

9. I am resourceful and capable. ☐

Explain:

10. I express my needs and stand by my values without guilt. ☐

Explain:

Observe which statements above you ranked higher than 3. These are the experiences, ideas, and attitudes that are **directly contributing to your ongoing growth and personal achievement.** If you ranked most areas more than 3, congratulations! Maintain consistency in these areas and strive to raise any you ranked less than a 3 by continuing your quest for self-discovery and improvement.

A boundary is something that you will do or not do based on a specific circumstance that may involve a person or situation. As you consider your boundaries, think of your values, too.

If one of your values includes working for a company with integrity, what would you do if someone asked you to steal? Would it vary by situation? Stealing can mean taking something tangible that is not yours to charging somebody more than what is expected because you know they can afford it.

For parents, consider the rules or boundaries you place on your children. Do you have a finite way you will handle lying, for example?

It is always better to think about and establish appropriate boundaries when you are emotionally neutral. It gives the unconscious a more appropriate response to go to when triggered versus one that might be based on high-charged emotions like anger, fear, or desperation.

## 4 Steps of Boundary Setting

- First, you need to **Define Your Boundaries** – Identifying and communicating boundaries and consequences is empowering and creates trusting relationships.

- Next, you must **Set Your Boundaries** – Now that you have identified your boundaries while in a clear headspace; it's time to explain and set them via proper communication.

- Third, and the hardest for many people is **Enforcing Your Boundaries** – Upholding the consequences of boundary violation.

- Finally, **Respect the Boundaries of Other People** – Help others communicate their needs, and respect them when they do to create mutual trust and integrity.

When deciding to enforce boundaries there are a few things to consider:

1. How is it going to affect you?
2. Is your consequence spiteful, harmful, or unnecessarily punishing?
3. Are you willing to lose a relationship?
4. Are you prepared to leave to protect your well-being?

Consider these items when doing the following exercise.

# Boundary Setting

<u>Instructions</u>

Using the examples below, identify a few situations in your life where you know you have not stood by what is best for you. Consider each of the Sectors of Self to help you narrow your focus: *Health & Fitness; Relationships; Friends & Family; Personal Growth & Development; Career & Finances; and Spirituality.*

Please note that everyone's boundaries are different and the examples below are illustrations.

### Example 1 – Friends

1. **Define:** You run into your neighbor while out on a weekend and see him romantically involved with a woman who is not his wife (your good friend) and you know they do not have an open relationship. He begs you not to say anything to his wife, but you do not intend to keep his lie.

**Possible challenges you must be willing to accept:** Neighbor gets angry and calls you all sorts of names. Friend gets mad at you because she doesn't believe you, or blames you. Loss of friendship.

2. **Set:** Explain to the neighbor that he has until a specific day to tell his wife, or you are going to.

3. **Enforce:** If the friend has not already told you her husband confessed, stand by your word to disclose the affair by the specified date, reminding the neighbor that you intend to do so several days in advance.

### Example 2 – Family

1. **Define:** You discover your daughter has been lying to you about various topics, and she knows that lying is not acceptable in your home. You have already asked yourself why she feels she must lie to you. Is it her behavior or is she afraid of you?

**Possible challenges you must be willing to accept:** A lot of screaming. Storming out. Threats intended to hurt your feelings or scare you.

2. **Set:** Ask your daughter why she fears coming to you with the truth and address the answer. Explain the consequences of continued lying. The next violation is the loss of her mobile device for three days; the second violation is the loss of car privileges; and the third violation is she is fully grounded with no social privileges for the following two weekends and after school.

3. **Enforce:** Stand by the escalating consequences of each violation.

### Example 3 – Career

1. **Define:** Your boss has been calling you every Saturday morning for weeks and you find yourself doing hours of work at her whim because she asked you to, even though the company talks about work/life balance all the time. There is no special project, she just doesn't have boundaries of her own with work.

**Possible challenges you must be willing to accept:** Your boss will be irritated. You fall out of favor with the boss. You finally have enough and leave the company.

2. **Set:** Next time she calls, explain to her that you will give her a set number of hours on that day only but are no longer going to spend your weekends doing work because she has decided she wants to. Remind her that everyone needs personal time like the company claims and stand by your need for it.

3. **Enforce:** If she calls again don't answer the phone or reply to her emails until work hours.

---

### Situation 1

1. Define:




Possible challenges you must be willing to accept:




2. Set:




3. Enforce:



---

**<u>Situation 2</u>**

1.  Define: .......................................................................................................................
.............................................................................................................................................
.............................................................................................................................................

Possible challenges you must be willing to accept: ...............................................
.............................................................................................................................................
.............................................................................................................................................

2.  Set: ...........................................................................................................................
.............................................................................................................................................
.............................................................................................................................................

3.  Enforce: ...................................................................................................................
.............................................................................................................................................
.............................................................................................................................................

**<u>Situation 3</u>**

1.  Define: .......................................................................................................................
.............................................................................................................................................
.............................................................................................................................................

Possible challenges you must be willing to accept: ...............................................
.............................................................................................................................................
.............................................................................................................................................

2.  Set: ...........................................................................................................................
.............................................................................................................................................
.............................................................................................................................................

3.  Enforce: ...................................................................................................................
.............................................................................................................................................

# TENET 7

# COMMUNICATION

**Themes:**

- Hearing content through delivery so you can reflect back information and emotion.
- Learning to fully engage in effective, quality conversation.

**Exercise Topics:** *Active Listening*

Below you will find the example statement from "FEELING STUCK?" and a reminder of how to use the 4 Techniques of Active Listening.

**Example Statement:** We went to Spain and England. It was awesome then sucked. The first week in Spain was great. Then I got a bad flu in London and spent the final five days of the vacation in the hotel.

## 4 Techniques of Active Listening/Mirroring

1. **Paraphrasing.** Briefly summarizing what you heard in your own words. (i.e., "It sounds like your trip was a real mixed bag of highs and lows depending on the city.")

2. **Reflecting Feelings.** Expressing back the feelings you heard them say or have interpreted. (i.e., "Sounds like you were pretty bummed during the last half of your trip.")

3. **Relating Feelings to Content.** Connecting the feelings heard to the facts given. (i.e., "So basically, you are saying that Spain was amazing but you're pretty disappointed you didn't get to enjoy London.")

4. **Clarifying.** Clearing up any confusion with open-ended (i.e., "How did you realize you couldn't push through and explore London?") and closed-ended questions (i.e., "Were you the only person who got sick?" "Were you stuck in the hotel alone?").

Since it is often difficult to come up with nuanced feelings to describe how you feel or what you may have heard, below is a list of feelings words to help you accurately describe your feelings, or when relating feelings and content.

# Often Overlooked Feelings Words

| | | | |
|---|---|---|---|
| Abandoned | Devastated | Hurt | Rage |
| Afraid | Disconnected | Ignored | Rejected |
| Agonized | Disheartened | Imposed Upon | Relieved |
| Ambivalent | Distracted | Infuriated | Sad |
| Angry | Empty | Intimidated | Scared |
| Annoyed | Envious | Isolated | Shocked |
| Anxious | Fearful | Left Out | Stunned |
| Betrayed | Foolish | Lonely | Tense |
| Bitter | Frightened | Low | Terrible |
| Burdened | Frustrated | Miserable | Threatened |
| Cheated | Furious | Out of Control | Tired |
| Confused | Guilty | Outraged | Trapped |
| Crossed | Helpless | Overwhelmed | Unsettled |
| Crushed | Homesick | Panicked | Vulnerable |
| Defeated | Hopeless | Pressured | Worried |

# Active Listening

<u>Instructions</u>

Use the following statements to practice your active listening skills. Examples of responses are included with each statement. Your responses may vary.

---

**1. "I wonder if I do too much for my husband. He doesn't do much for me or anyone else. I prepped the whole house for the upcoming holiday, and he didn't do a thing to help."**

Paraphrasing:

Feelings:

Reflective Feelings Statement:

Relating Feelings to Content:

∞

**Paraphrasing:** You are saying you do too much and think your husband is lazy or selfish.

**Feelings:** Unloved, undervalued, underappreciated

**Reflective Feelings Statement**: I sense you are feeling unloved and underappreciated, perhaps sad or used.

**Relating Feelings to Content:** Listening to you, it seems that while you know your husband has a pattern you are feeling undervalued or sad, especially since you think you may be doing too much for him.

---

2. **"I don't like undressing in front of my spouse. I hate showing my body."**

Paraphrasing: ...................................................................................................

.......................................................................................................................

.......................................................................................................................

Feelings: ............................................................................................................

.......................................................................................................................

.......................................................................................................................

Reflective Feelings Statement: .........................................................................

.......................................................................................................................

.......................................................................................................................

Relating Feelings to Content: ...........................................................................

.......................................................................................................................

.......................................................................................................................

∞

**Paraphrasing:** Your body image concerns are affecting your relationship.

**Feelings:** Unhappy, low self-esteem, disgusted, insecure, uncomfortable

**Reflective Feelings Statement:** It sounds like you are uncomfortable with your body.

**Relating Feelings to Content:** I'm hearing you say that your discomfort with your body is creating a barrier between you and your spouse.

3. **"I'm only going to therapy because my wife is making me. It's a waste of time. She has the problems, not me."**

Paraphrasing:

Feelings:

Reflective Feelings Statement:

Relating Feelings to Content:

∞

**Paraphrasing:** You are going to therapy because your wife wants you to but you have no interest and think it's a waste of time.

**Feelings:** Irritated, annoyed, pressured, frustrated, out of control

**Reflective Feelings Statement:** You seem really irritated.

**Relating Feelings to Content:** What I'm hearing you say is that you are feeling forced to do something you don't want to do, about problems you don't feel are yours.

4. **"I'm running away from home. Nothing I do is ever right. Besides, they just want me there so they can tell me what to do."**

Paraphrasing:

Feelings:

Reflective Feelings Statement:

Relating Feelings to Content:

∞

**Paraphrasing:** Your parents ask a lot of you, but you are never right or good enough anyway, so you want to leave.

**Feelings:** Helpless, underappreciated, unloved, used, rejected, annoyed, not good enough

**Reflective Feelings Statement:** It sounds like you feel like you are not good enough, as well as annoyed and underappreciated.

**Relating Feelings to Content:** What I'm hearing you say is that you feel you aren't good enough because you are often told you are never right yet have a lot of pressure on you to do a lot for the family anyway.

5. **"I am so tired of everyone being promoted before me at work. I have been there forever, work hard and know what I'm doing. I'm wondering if it's just my age. I'm so done but don't have many options at this point."**

Paraphrasing:

Feelings:

Reflective Feelings Statement:

Relating Feelings to Content:

∞

**Paraphrasing:** Even though you are a top-notch worker you keep getting overlooked for promotions and see options lessening as you get older.

**Feelings:** Exhausted, exasperated, hopeless, insecure, overlooked, rejected, confident

**Reflective Feelings Statement:** It sounds like you are confident in your skills and are feeling rejected and hopeless at the same time.

**Relating Feelings to Content:** Though you know you are very capable and a great worker, it seems you believe there is some injustice at work regarding promotions, and you feel like you might be trapped there waiting with few options because of your age.

Now, it is time for you to practice your active listening skills in your everyday life. When you are with a friend or family, use the steps you just learned to become fully engaged in the conversation. Keep it simple to start, paraphrase. From there, begin to incorporate the feelings words you heard. Take notice of how the quality of your conversations improves.

# WELLNESS

---

**Themes:**

- Evaluating how you practice self-care, and how balanced you are between caring for others and yourself.
- Assisting you in managing your self-care with a calendar tracking tool.

**Exercise Topics:** *Self-Care Evaluation, Wellness Commitment Calendar*

---

## Self-Care Evaluation

1. Do you focus on taking care of other people, yourself only, or a balance of both?

How does this positively and negatively affect you?

2. In the last three months, how would you describe your mental, emotional, and physical vibrancy? Why do you think that is so?

3.  Do you remember a time when your mental and emotional energy and physical vibrancy were at their best? How did that feel and what was going on then?

4.  In the areas of nutrition, exercise, mindfulness, and sleep, what habits do you routinely follow that support your overall health and well-being?

5.  What routines do you have for recharging daily, weekly, monthly, and yearly?

6.  What frequent habits would increase your everyday energy, and what types of retreats, vacations, or staycations would help reset you?

7.  Are there any areas of your life that are particularly stressful or draining energetically? If so, what are they, and have you been trying to manage the stress or simply avoid it?

8. In order to be more committed to your optimal health, what would you immediately start doing and stop doing?

# Wellness Commitment Calendar

Instructions

Use the calendar below to track self-care habits. You can refer to the Wellness Commitment Checklist from "FEELING STUCK?" for examples related to activity, energizing, and mindfulness.

**Goals:**

- ✓ **Sleep:** 7-9 hours/day
- ✓ **Activity:** 30 min./day, 4x/week minimum
- ✓ **Meals:** 5-6/day
- ✓ **Water:** Minimum 64 oz./day to 1 oz./pound of body weight
- ✓ **Daily energizing:** Minimum 5 min./day
- ✓ **Mindfulness:** Minimum 5 min./day

| Week of: | SUN | MON | TUE | WED | THUR | FRI | SAT |
|---|---|---|---|---|---|---|---|
| Hours of Sleep: | | | | | | | |
| Activity Time/Type: | | | | | | | |
| Meals/Day: | | | | | | | |
| Water Qty/Day: | | | | | | | |
| Daily Energizing Time/Type: | | | | | | | |
| Mindfulness Time/Type: | | | | | | | |

| Week of: | SUN | MON | TUE | WED | THUR | FRI | SAT |
|---|---|---|---|---|---|---|---|
| Hours of Sleep: | | | | | | | |
| Activity Time/Type: | | | | | | | |
| Meals/Day: | | | | | | | |
| Water Qty/Day: | | | | | | | |
| Daily Energizing Time/Type: | | | | | | | |
| Mindfulness Time/Type: | | | | | | | |
| Week of: | SUN | MON | TUE | WED | THUR | FRI | SAT |
| Hours of Sleep: | | | | | | | |
| Activity Time/Type: | | | | | | | |
| Meals/Day: | | | | | | | |
| Water Qty/Day: | | | | | | | |
| Daily Energizing Time/Type: | | | | | | | |
| Mindfulness Time/Type: | | | | | | | |

# TENET 9
# MODELING

**Themes:**

- Determining how you want to be a model of excellence and for whom.
- Deciding what you will need to learn, how you can grow and encourage growth, and in what ways you will inspire.

**Exercise Topics:** *Learn. Grow. Inspire.*®

---

The most influential people are pillars of growth and sponges for knowledge. They lead by example both directly and indirectly. Role models challenge people to look beyond their attitudes and beliefs about self and others and inspire a personal quest for excellence. People model those they respect, who show up, and who take action. One of the mantras of Mindset Transformation Coaching® is *Learn. Grow. Inspire.*® and it is through this process that the most influential people create the most impact.

Learning creates personal growth, and as you grow you directly and passively influence and inspire others. There will be times when you learn to further your growth and other times when you learn to help further the growth of other people.

# Learn. Grow. Inspire.®

Instructions

Please provide your answers to the concepts below.

## LEARN

Having a thirst for knowledge and growth demonstrates to others that you never stop growing or learning no matter how successful or abundant life is. While you may plateau at times, no one person has reached their capacity for further wisdom, resolve, compassion, or empathy. This is your demonstration to the world that you are willing to keep bettering yourself, and that there is always something new to learn or model.

1. What do I need to learn, however big or small, to grow as a person?

2.  The reasons I am willing to learn about new topics to grow as a person are...

### *Think of a person or group you would like to influence.*

(This can be related to any area of your life. Work, family, friends, community.)

1.  Where do I wish I had more influence in my life right now?

*Example: New work colleagues*

2.  What I can do to increase my influence in that area...

*Example: Show up on time, be eager, and ask quality questions that show I want more knowledge.*

3.  If I am going to have more influence, I will need to learn about these topics to be in rapport and earn their respect...

*Example: Learn about the positions that interact with mine so I can understand how they can best influence each other.*

4. I am currently showing up for them by...

*Example: Doing the best job I can for my position.*

5. I can improve how I show up for them by...

*Example: Offering to take on a leadership role for other people learning the same position.*

# GROW

Once you have the necessary tools and knowledge it is up to you to use those items to encourage personal growth in those you lead.

**Think of a different person or group you would like to influence or use the same as above.**

**Person or group:** _____ **(Ex. School volleyball team)**

1. In what ways will the person or group I want to influence need to grow? (It can be as specific as an isolated skill, or as broad as a changed perspective.)

*Example: The school volleyball team I coach needs to trust each other more on the court.*

2.  This growth will benefit them by...

*Example: It will help plays run more smoothly because the person who is supposed to get to the ball will be able to without interference unless she asks for help.*

3.  I can demonstrate the possible future outcomes this growth will create by...

*Example: Showing examples of winning teams who play as a cohesive unit where everyone does their job and supports each other.*

4.  I will get them excited to step outside of their comfort zone and learn the necessary knowledge, skills, or abilities to create these outcomes by...

*Example: Using drills that show each person that they can get to almost any ball, how to call for help if needed, and trust that someone will ask for help rather than jeopardizing the play.*

5.  To be successful, I will need to get them to believe the following...

*Example: Each person will do their very best and they must let them do their job, while trusting that each person will call for help if needed.*

# INSPIRE

Inspiring others happens passively from natural observation of your growth, as well as by directly choosing to step up in service, and lead as a model of excellence.

***Think of a different person or group you would like to influence or use the same as above.***

**Person or group:** _____ **(ex. My kids)**

1.  In order to inspire this person or group I will need to have these values…

*Example: The ability to listen to their needs and opinions and not demand only what I want. Come from a place of education, remembering that I have more life experience than they do.*

2.  I demonstrate that excellence does not mean perfection in these ways…

*Example: Apologize when I react too firmly.*

3.  I will need to use my confidence and communication in these ways in order to influence these people…

*Example: Though still the house leader, I can create an environment where I help the kids learn to stand up for themselves while being respectful, to me and their siblings.*

4.  I will need to step up in these ways to inspire them…

*Example: Be proactive in advancing their independence by having them take on more confidence-building responsibility. Be more genuinely interested in what goes on in their day rather than viewing it as kid stuff.*

# TENET 10
# **PURPOSE**

---

**Themes:**

- Creating a personal code of conduct.
- Defining who you are as a person and what you will need to do to have congruency with your core values.

**Exercise Topics:** *Creating Your Purpose Statement*

---

You have probably noticed, most businesses, especially large ones, have a mission statement as part of their core identity. It helps them stay aligned with their values as they maneuver in the global economy. A personal mission statement, or purpose statement, is similar — it is a single sentence that sums up who you are, what your values are, and how your legacy will impact the world. This is a fundamental exercise and guiding force to define your life's purpose and how you serve those around you. It is not uncommon to have different statements of purpose for family or work, or any of the Sectors of Self.

Your purpose statement may change as you age, experience life, and grow. It is okay to give yourself permission to do so since change is fundamental to growth. Know that no matter what it says, living each day with vitality, presence, and meaning is the ultimate goal.

Below you will create your purpose statement. Think of it as a broad code of conduct. Your statement should be in alignment with your values and answer questions like the following:

1. **Who am I?** This may define some of your core characteristics.
2. **Who do I want to become?** Spiritually, intellectually, emotionally, and physically.
3. **What do I want to do?** What accomplishments do you seek?
4. **How do I want to act?** What kind of behavior do you want to showcase?
5. **What do I represent?** How would you want people to describe you?
6. **Who do I want to best serve?** What community do you want to positively influence?
7. **Why are these things important to me?** How do these align with your core values?
8. **What do I want for my legacy?** How would you want your life's summary described?

Great purpose statements help people define their value and their moral code. Having a thoughtful statement in place makes tough decisions much easier because you've already defined a personal boundary.

Reminders:

1. **Keep it short and/or simple.** This is your "elevator pitch" that describes what you represent in a simple fashion.
2. **Use a verb to describe your "be/do" in the beginning.** Start with what you want to be or do.
3. **How will you impact others?** The statement represents you and the people you influence.
4. **Let it evolve with you.** The statement will evolve with you but stay rooted in your fundamental values.

Examples:

"To create a kind, patient, and supportive environment for my family, employees, and customers."

"To engage the elderly in community service and continued life purpose."

"To be a supportive influence by showing up for everyone I meet in order to positively impact their lives."

"To demonstrate spiritual non-judgment so that people everywhere feel safe in their personal expression."

"To continue exploring better ways to lessen the negative global impact created by our carbon footprint and create a more sustainable environment for generations to come."

# Creating Your Purpose Statement

Instructions

Before you begin, find a quiet place and clear your mind. Be sure to write from your heart and be genuine about what you truly represent or will achieve. If it feels right to you, even if the little voice is unsure, trust your gut. Remember, purpose statements are broad, they are not goals.

1. The statement can have elements of "being" or "doing." For example, my statement includes "be a seeker of knowledge and never-ending growth," which is a broad statement that represents me in all areas of life.

*I would like my purpose statement to demonstrate who I am and include...*

2.  The statement can also have an action verb demonstrating what you want to do. For example, my statement includes "understanding other people's model of the world." Empathy and learning about what drives and limits other people is part of who I am.

*I would like my purpose statement to remind me to do...*

```



```

3.  The statement might also have a "so that" or "in order to" element to describe why you want to be or do those things. This might be about any of the Sectors of Self or relate to you broadly. For example, my statement about my career includes "so that I can encourage others to realize the power each person has to maximize their life fulfillment and joy."

*The reason I wrote the above "be" and "do" elements in my purpose statement is...*

```



```

Bring your responses for 1 to 3 together into one purpose statement. For example, my purpose statement is "The purpose of my life is to be a seeker of knowledge and never-ending growth, with a commitment to understanding other people's model of the world, so that I can encourage others to realize the power each person has to maximize their life fulfillment and joy." While that statement is largely about who I am in my career, it also represents me at a fundamental level. I could make minor modifications to the last part to represent any other area of my personal life more directly.

## *My Purpose Statement is...*

Remember, this statement is your guiding force and generally defines what you stand for and how you live your life. Keep it somewhere you can look at it daily and share it with the people around you.

# Closing Thoughts

Congratulations! You have completed the exercises that accompany your Mindset Transformation Coaching® program. If you did skip a few, I encourage you to do them when you are ready but without too much delay. It's the coherence that makes long-term growth most sustainable.

Moving forward, I encourage you to revisit topics where you need the most help and any topic where you know you have grown the most. That way you will see your evolution. Consider how you can apply your success from the areas of most growth to other areas where you might be sluggish. As a model of excellence, consider sharing exercises like Values Elicitation and Active Listening. They are always relevant and excellent to use in regular life practice, especially with other people.

Keep in mind, you are always growing and changing. You might decide to revisit "FEELING STUCK?" and its companion workbook at a future time and discover that your insight and awareness changed, and therefore how you answered the questions changed as well. Personal empowerment, happiness, and life fulfillment look different to everyone, including new versions of yourself — and that is what you are becoming!

Change your mindset. Change your life.®

*Nicole*

# About the Author

Nicole hosts workshops and online events, coaches privately, and speaks at private and public conferences and organizations. Her topics include the importance of using your voice and quality communication, values, overcoming obstacles and limiting beliefs, confidence and boundary setting, general nutrition, and the pursuit of life balance and fulfillment. She tailors each engagement to her audience.

She is board certified by the Association for Integrative Psychology in Mental and Emotional Release® (MER), Neuro Linguistic Programming (NLP) and Hypnotherapy, the American Council on Exercise, and the OSHA Training Institute.

To book Nicole for **keynote and other speaking events, workshops,** or **team development training** contact:

support@nicolehollar.com

To learn more about **Mindset Transformation Breakthrough Coaching** and other resources visit:

www.nicolehollar.com

@nicolehollarcoaching